Moonlight Musings

Love, Life & Poetry

Constance Wah

BookLeaf Publishing

Presentation by *BookLeaf Publishing*

Web: www.bookleafpub.com

E-mail: info@bookleafpub.com

ISBN: 978-93-5721-655-5

First edition 2023

For Chacey, our bambino.

ACKNOWLEDGEMENTS

My heartfelt thanks to my parents, sisters, family, and friends for all their love and support. My immense gratitude to BookLeaf Publishing and of course to you my dear readers. If your heart feels like breaking, know that your pain is only meant to make you stronger.

PREFACE

It was right before Christmas of 2021 when my sister, May, registered my name to the 21-day Writing Challenge out of the blue. I guess she recognized a boredom in me curable only by such an adventure. This book is a product of that poetic journey. My life is not a linear narrative. It's a concoction of a variety of elements that shaped me to be the person that I am today. This book is a collection I made over the years, and most were written during the pandemic in the dead of night when everything was silent save for the rumblings of my innermost thoughts. This serves as a reflection of my life's journey through the seasons that passed - the joy of being in love, the crushing heartbreaks, the loss of a loved one, the struggles of being a woman, the highs and lows, and the moments worth celebrating. These past couple years have been a rollercoaster ride for most of us. The events brought about by the pandemic certainly made me look at life in a new light.

For people like me who keep to themselves, sometimes our weapon is the pen and our refuge poetry - for written words convey what we cannot say. Cheers to you!

Constance

msconstancew@gmail.com

Through the Storm

Storms come in many forms
Some are mild, others turbulent and fierce
Life is an endless sea of possibilities.
When the skies are red in the morning,
That's when sailors take warning.
When the skies are red at night,
That's when sailors delight.

You'll be surprised
At the clues nature gives you.
But as you journey towards the tempest,
The raging waves will beat you up
Like the pounding of a battering ram.
The thunder's roar will shake your core

And the wild wind will pummel its heavy
fists
Until you're knocked out.

You'll never know
What life will throw at you.
But my friend, please remember
Even when your boat feels like tipping over
And the weary mast is about to surrender…
There's a beacon of light beyond the horizon
And the unseen hand of your Captain
will guide your sails to the safety of the
dry land.

Bubble

All that I cherish
and hold dear
I'll fervently include
in my humble prayer.

All that I treasure
and hold dear
I'll enclose in a bubble
and keep safe even if I'm not there.

The world can be cruel and unfair
It's one of life's despair
To be away from people
in need of your care.

All that I love
and hold dear
I'll wrap inside my heart
and carry with me everywhere.

Slow Dance

One, two, three...
One, two, three...
And so, it went on like a summer breeze.
Our hands clasped together
My palm nestled warmly upon your shoulder.
We flowed with the gentle curves of the river.

The pleasant beat lulled us into a soft trance.
Our rhythm was perfect in that slow dance.
We floated high up in the wispy clouds
Then fell gently back to the ground
Swaying side by side,
Waltzing through the night.

Brown Eyes

Hold me...
Your gaze holds me with the gripping force
of someone pulling on the opposite end of
the rope.
The strength of your fiery stare burns me.
In this tug of war, you beat me.

Hold me...
You look at me in a way
that makes my heart sway.
Those brown eyes gaze at me... so far away
but it's enough to make me stay.

‘Cause It’s You

One night, one dance felt like forever.
I wished we could be together.
It seems like a decade hasn’t passed.
I’m staring at your brown eyes, at last.

How can it be?
Your gaze still pierces through me.
It’s surreal how you still make me feel.
Our hearts in a box,
wrapped until fate brought us back.

Can this be real?
‘cause it’s you
Love comes easily.

‘cause it’s you
Love comes naturally.

I see, between red and yellow in hue,
there is only you.

Restless

It's when the dark skies are littered
with the luster of stars,
when the wistful wind blows its long,
weary sigh...
These woeful thoughts start seeping in
through quietude; they crawl uninvited
as unwelcome guests persist like pests.

Severed

I hate for these wounds
to incubate, grow, and fester.
I can't bear the searing soreness any longer.
The nights are drenched with tears of sorrow.
It's hard to see the promise of tomorrow.

I always thought
that love would last forever.
But sadly…
You're no longer
the same person I remember.

It's hard to let go…
when you don't know how to.
It's hard to let go…
when you really don't want to.

But you're no longer
the same person I remember.

Now, it’s so much better
for this losing game to be over.

This...

This…
regretful longing
This…
silent suffering
This…
wishful thinking
This…
Lonely heart beating,
pining only
for you.

Pendulum

While half the world is asleep,
this pensive mood settles in
drawing melancholy into the deepest
crevices and labyrinths of my mind.
A weary soul gazes up at the moon.
One expects calm, only to be dismayed.
She pulls the tides of the roaring seas
stirring torment to an ebbing grief.

The one I asked God to keep safe each night
may he see a Ray of light - do what's right.
Though the rain may be heavy,
it'll let up, surely.
Of the blazing fire what remains are embers
Will time rekindle or help salve and heal?
A force so strong that even the wisest fall.

Now, I fear - its shard severs, its strength
breaks
I watch the pendulum come to a halt
So will my weary heart come to rest.

Unrequited Love

Perhaps there is no consolation
in the unfortunate occasion
when one earnestly yearns for another
but that someone doesn't even bother.

Perhaps you shouldn't search for
someone a poet conjured from a lore
It's a futile attempt to hope for
something that never even existed before.

La Luna

Tonight, she draws closer than ever
Although her glow is not hers to show
at her zenith - her fullest, her brightest
a magnificent version of herself.

She takes the reins
driving her glowing chariot,
drawn by mighty white horses
across the skies each night.

Draped and embellished, beautiful in white,
her cathedral train flowing endlessly
bathing one captured soul in all that
glorious light
soaking up, basking in with pure delight.

How one adores her mighty strength
She pulls the tides of tempestuous seas
not for a moment was it Poseidon's
for even the dreamy sea isn't its own master
They bend the knee before her.

Hard Shell

Any stranger would heed,
The barricades - unyielding, indeed.
Those four frosty walls - steadfast and
stately
Those silky strands spun around her
Every fiber makes it stronger
Draped in a cocoon to protect her,
thus an uninviting fortress
Dreadful to tread, frightful to trespass.

As time passes on like a long sigh,
she grows within that shiny shell
There will never be
The beauty nor the luster of a jewel
Without the unwelcome prod
Perhaps we'll never know.

In her own time, she blossoms, opens up
There's so much more to her than that
Lo and behold, deep within her hard shell
She cradles a precious pearl.

- *(Recounting my first meeting with my friend, Jamaica)*

Fairies

Fairies are real; I have two.
From sharing laughters to wiping tears,
lucky are those who have one.
Without the both of you,
I wouldn't have a clue
Worse, I would be blue.

It's not just the blood
warmly rushing through our veins -
not only the same genes.
Apart we are weak, like a hydrogen bond.
Neither covalent nor ionic will do.
By heart, strongly bound our strings are.

Fairies are real; I have two.
You help make my dreams come true.
Blessed I am to have sisters like you.

Bambino

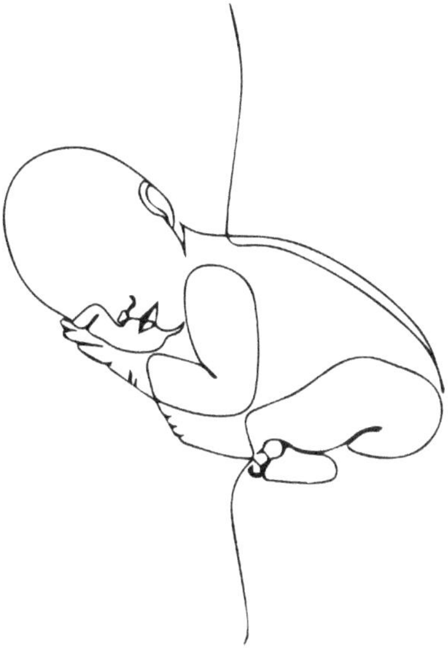

We have waited for so long
On bended knees
We fervently prayed
And the good Lord answered.

Our hearts truly desired
For you, bambino
That heaven saw how badly
We wanted you.

Our hearts were filled
With gladness and cheer

When you came to us
Wrapped in a cuddly bear.

The calming scent of lavender in your curly hair
Fills the misty November air
This lovely cherub loves his bag of feathers
And got us all wrapped around his little finger.

What Might Have Been

It's Christmastime again
I look back on the years passed
And the "*what might have beens*"
are in its own class.

It's a mysterious thing
All the wise men have wondered
How to undo something
you wished had never happened.

There's no sense in longing
for something that might have been

All the lost times have vanished
Never to be caught again.

Words

Where do I start?
For there are so many…
Some are nice, others mean at times
It's a wonder you ran out of things to say
when your mind is a speedy freeway.

The words will slowly flow
like they did two nights ago
But when you decide to speak,
make it a kind word or two
With a smile on the lips, also.

Books

There's a magical portal
That leads me to places
I've never been.
I hold out my hand
And with every page
I'm transported in an instant.
Each new adventure is a surprise
Every time I open my eyes.

Tambobo Bay

The northeast monsoon winds
bring a melody of melancholy
The cool November air whispers pensively
"Where are you, amore mio?"

Beyond the steep rocks sprawling vastly
the stage juts out proudly on a ledge
Embracing the soft rays of light
in this cozy, tropical paradise.

Where the rugged edges meet
the endless turquoise sea
And the slopes peppered with
the vibrant blush of bougainvillea blossoms
There echoes the drumming beat

of a lonely frigate bird
Calling for his mate
as she glides high in the blue skies.

Rise up!
The calm sea beckons you
Look out the open window
That view is perfect with you.

Rise up!
Hear the waves lapping against the pebbled shores
Across the majestic cliffs lies a gateway
An abyss of freedom lay beyond the bay.

Death

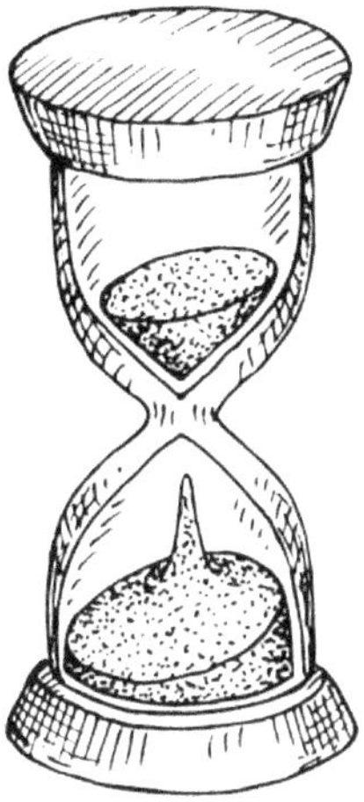

It is one of life's greatest ironies
That people only listen to you
When you're dead…
When the wind has taken away
Even the faintest whispers,
To be showered with flowers
When you're no longer
Able to appreciate their scent
Or make amends
When it's already too late.

Angel in the Shadows

What would you have done differently
If you knew it was for the last time?
Would you turn that anger into laughter?
That courteous nod into a long embrace?
Would you hold that hand a little longer
And hope it lasts forever?

The Angel in the shadows
Though looked upon with sorrow
Is not really your foe.
In all of life's endless possibilities
In the end…
It remains the only certainty.

That friend in the shadows
Won't say when it'll meet you
"*One day*" is all they say

Though some are still lucky
For they are somehow privy
To their timely rendezvous.

To those who
still have time to love,
Love fiercely!
And to those who
still have time to live,
Live fully!

As you wake up with the morning dew
Refreshed and new
Add a spring in your steps
And a melody in your lips
Knowing that with every breath
You have been blessed.

Last Dance

After every door that closes,
Another opens.
Don't despair!
For it's only with the lack of trying
That you're doomed to fail.

Make the first step
Towards your goal
And give it your best
It's an opportunity
You wouldn't want to miss.

Make the most
Of every given chance
For you'll never know
If it's your last dance.

Living in a Fast World

We drive through this
Fast-paced existence
In a Bugatti Chiron...
We run past the stop signs
That were never meant
To be ignored.
Everyone is always in a rush
To be somewhere in a flash.

We no longer take the time
To pause and admire
The beauty of the ocean.
So often we forget that
The best moments in life
Were meant to be savored
Bit by bit with every part
Of our conscious being.

Whirlwind

I took another chance
And opened up my heart
For a second time
I didn't have time to think
You just swept me off my feet.

You were irresistibly charming
The words you whispered
Were calming and soothing
You revived my once grieving heart
And had me hoping,
Dreaming once again.

Empty Promises

You only craved for
The warmth of these arms
That hold you close.

You delight in the thought
Of someone longing
And pining for you.

You take it all
But you never give back
As much in return.

You only love the concept of being in love
But your words were empty
When you said you loved me.

You never really loved me, anyway.

Bleed

If my heart were made of glass,
It would have shattered
Into a thousand pieces.

But I am only human
Organic and raw
With these wounds, I bleed too.

Potion

(An antidote for a broken heart)

If moving on was as easy
As drinking a potion,
If that's a guaranteed remedy,
I probably would have had already
Concocted my own quick recipe
No matter how elusive
The ingredients may be.

Love is a test sometimes
Only the brave survive the loss
Vie to be faithful
Even in this superficial world.

Sometimes, I scream in silence
Trying to get through the day
Realizing that life can be tougher, at times
Even for those who got it all figured out
So much is still required
So I tell myself to press on and survive.

Hustle

Everyone is hustling
like crazy.
Not me.
I guess I'm just lazy.
But health is my
first priority.
So I'll just sit back
and try not to worry.
At the end of the day,
all will be okay.

Upset the World

In order to make a change,
You have to make some noise first
And be the trouble you're
Destined to be.
You'll get nowhere
If you stay where you are
Set out to travel
Upset the world and turn it
upside down.

Surgery

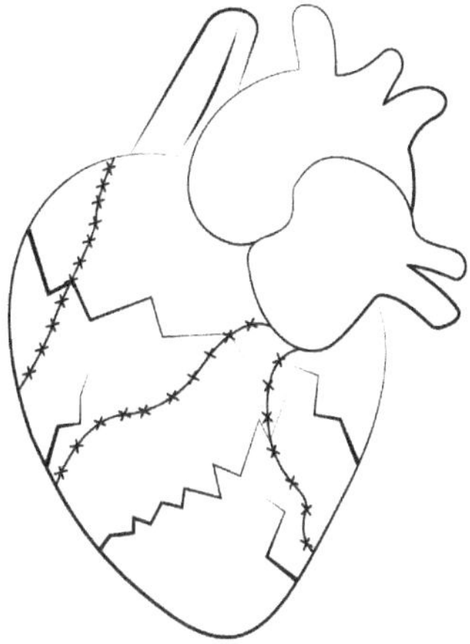

When you look at people
And you don't like what you see
Every time you call someone ugly
Or think that they need work on their body
So they can look pretty
Based on your standards of beauty
Remember that at the end of the day
It's your heart
That needs surgery.

Free

Have you ever wondered
What it feels like to spread your
Wings wide and fly until
The world beneath you
Is nothing but a landscape
Your eyes marvel at?

The sparrows never had to worry
About what others might say,
Or where the next meal may be,
Or cared as much if a feather was
Out of place or not.

Let go of the things that bother you.
You don't need anyone's opinion
To validate your value.

Choosing to be free of worry
Is the key to truly being free.

Home

It feels so helpless to be lost
With no sense of direction
When you're in constant search for home.

There's this air of foreboding
When life starts to question its own
meaning.
It's been so long since that fateful journey
Brought me to the land of milk and honey.
But the taste was bittersweet.
Each year that passed morphed into a cold,
steel bar
That my hands gripped until they're numb.
The gilded cage starts to feel like prison.

When will I see the Sun with the stars
around it?
The palm trees are waving "*hello*"
Home... oh how I've missed you!
I want to know if you still wave the banner
of your peaceful blue.

Motherland

She
wears
the
blazing sun
for
a crown.

Nothing
can
take her
down.

She

She
Was a woman
Way ahead
Of her time.

She
Was brainy
But they couldn't
See past her beauty.

She
Was the maker
Of her own
Grand destiny.

Liberty

The women of today
Can be anyone they want to be.
They're no longer bound
By rules dictated by society.
Sadly, some parts of the world
Are still living in the 19th century.
So the fight goes on
Until everyone gets the same
Liberty.

- *This piece is dedicated to the brave Nasrin Sotoudeh and to all the warriors fighting not only for women's rights but also for upholding human rights and values as well.*

Solitude

I may be alone
but not lonely.
I'm mostly by myself
'cause I don't always
need company.

Being on your own
is a perfect time for reflection.
It's when you'll realize that
you only ever need
oxygen to breathe.

Once you've forgiven yourself
for always putting them first,
you'll know that you've been healed
and that all you ever really needed
was to love yourself first.

Table for One, Please

"A table for one, please."
Yes, at a sit-down restaurant
In the heart of town
Where you can hear the lively chatter
Of families and couples
Enjoying their meal together.

How I love food more than anything
Pure bliss with each scrumptious bite
I don't see what the big deal is
If you're dining on your own
To each her own.

Don't tell me that
You want to set me up
With someone who
Probably doesn't even want to.
Don't ask me if
I still plan to marry
If I wanted to, I would have done so
A long time ago.

Don’t say that it’s time for me
To have a child already
‘Cause we don’t need to be
Expectant to have a dozen babies
If being a mom is what we really
Dream to be.

Some can’t wrap their minds around
The idea that single people can
Still be happy even without
That special someone.

Shine Bright

Your shine is way more precious
Than the sparkle of a multifaceted
diamond ring
When price is gauged based on rarity
You are of most value, certainly
For there is no other quite like you.

Your whole being is made
Comparable to the dazzling of the
morning sun
Radiate all the positivity
That the world may lighten up
naturally with your
boundless energy.

Stewards

The Earth is home
To the gentle giants
That roam,
To the microbes
That thrive with you
Since you were born.

The Earth is home
To the greedy species
Who don't know
When to stop
Not until they have
Way more than enough.

The Earth is our only home
Though we are not
The rightful firstborn
We can still be loyal stewards
Of this majestic throne
And care for it
Not just for our own.

If I Were To Have a Daughter

They say that women will inherit the Earth
In all its glory and bounty
I find it quite hard to believe
Since the Bible wasn't even that nice to Eve
All they talk about is her famed temptation
But never her redemption.

So we navigate this unfair world
Traversing the paths while bound to our
curse
As some would like to say
"For the sins of our Mother, we must pay"
Is this why we have to stay?
To keep fighting for equality?

If I were to have a daughter,
May the world be kinder to her
May it be safer and fairer
I'll write an ode to our fallen sisters
That she may always remember
Her freedom was fought for by women of
valor.

She has risen up boldly

from the blazing flames

that should have burned her.

- **Constance Wah**

Haiku

Sad face or a frown
Laughter is the finest balm
Music to the soul.

Haiku

Life's full of struggles
The heart endures, with no choice
Keep moving forward.

Haiku

Death carries with it
Grief for the ones left behind
Repose for the soul.

Haiku

The past may haunt you,
But it does not define you
So just let it go.

Haiku

Where the flowers bloom,
Hope springs anew; love sprouts, too.
Only goodness grows.

A Cry in Broad Daylight

Yes, you heard it right.
There was a time when
Crimes were committed
In the dark of night
Away from plain sight.

Now we see all the stabbing,
Witness all the beating, harassing
These attackers are striking
In the middle of bustling cities
In front of our very eyes.

A wave of bullets
Rained ruthlessly
Upon the children
As they helplessly
Cried in broad daylight.

The world stands witness
To the untimely passing
Of the innocent lives
That fell prey to the
Vicious cycle of hate.

There's a vicarious trauma
From watching the news
Unfold in the media.
"Is my child safe from the
next shooting that will take place?"

The enemy likes to
Cause division
To broaden the chasm
Between people and nations
And to champion discrimination.

There's a constant fight
against this insanity - the disease
that cripples our society
Our hope lies within
The very core of our humanity.

What's born of violence
Will perish by the hand of violence
That's a pitiful way to end.
There's so much hatred
Driving people around the bend.

Our only hope is
Hanging by the thread
To recover the ability
To have a heart
And save humanity.

- *This piece is dedicated to the victims of hate crimes, the angels taken too soon by gun violence, and to the loved ones they left behind.*

Seeds

You can find kindness
In the most unusual places
You only have to look around
Or better yet
You can let it stem
From within
Let yourself be
A budding vessel
Let the bees pollinate
From the blooming
Flowers you planted
And as they sprinkle
Those precious seeds
Don't be surprised
To find goodness

Sprouting through
The cracked concrete
Of the city street.

www.ingramcontent.com/pod-product-compliance
Lightning Source LLC
Chambersburg PA
CBHW051734130826
49812CB00033B/862

* 9 7 8 9 3 5 7 2 1 6 5 5 5 *